Don't
Eat
Spiders

Poems by Robert Heidbreder • Pictures by Karen Patkau

Toronto Oxford

OXFORD UNIVERSITY PRESS

1985

CANADIAN CATALOGUING IN PUBLICATION DATA

Heidbreder, Robert.
Don't eat spiders
Poems.
ISBN 0-19-540497-1

1. Children's poetry, Canadian (English)*
I. Patkau, Karen.   II. Title.
PS8565.E43D66   1985   jC811'.54   C85-098792-X

OXFORD is a trademark of Oxford University Press
Poems © Robert Heidbreder 1985
Illustrations © Karen Patkau 1985
1 2 3 4 — 8 7 6 5
Printed and bound in Hong Kong by Scanner Art Services Inc., Toronto

Contents

4

A Big Bare Bear

A big bare bear
   bought a bear balloon,
For a big bear trip
   to the bare, bare moon.
A hairy bear
   saw the bare bear fly
On his big bear trip
   in the bare, bare sky.
The hairy bear
   took a jet up high
To catch the bear
   in the big bare sky.
The hairy bear
   flew his jet right by
The bear balloon
   in the big bare sky.
He popped the balloon
   with his hairy thumb,
And the bare bear fell
   on his big bum bum.

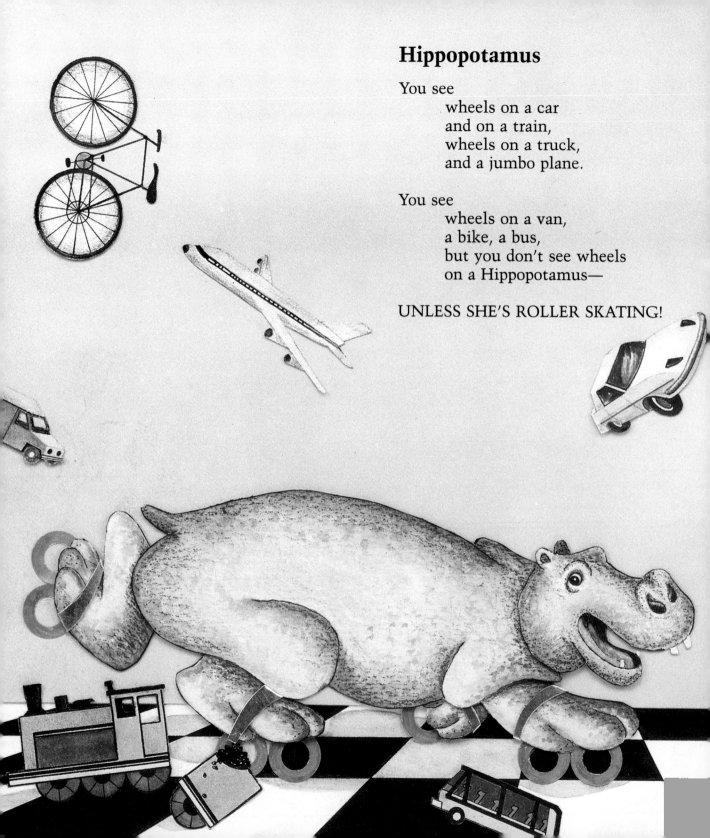

Hippopotamus

You see
    wheels on a car
    and on a train,
    wheels on a truck,
    and a jumbo plane.

You see
    wheels on a van,
    a bike, a bus,
    but you don't see wheels
    on a Hippopotamus—

UNLESS SHE'S ROLLER SKATING!

Little Robot

I'm a Little Robot,
    Wires make me talk.
I'm a Little Robot,
    Wires make me walk.
I'm a Little Robot,
    Wires bend my knees.
I'm a Little Robot,
    Wires make me sneeze.
        AAAACHOOOOOO!

I'm a Little Robot,
    Wires make me work.
So if you ever cross them,
    I'll probably go BERSERK!

ZOING ZOING BOINK!
ZOING ZOING BOINK!
ZING!

7

8

Sun, Sun

"Sun, Sun overhead,
What's your colour?"

"I am red."

"Sun, Sun, fiery fellow,
What's your colour?"

"I am yellow."

"Sun, Sun in sky of blue,
What's your colour?"

"Orange too.
I'm golden yellow,
Orange and red,
A burning fire above your head."

9

Falling Leaves

Swirling
    and twirling
        with flippity-flops
Down come the leaves from the tall treetops.

Floating
    and twisting
        around and around
Down come the leaves without a sound.

How to Catch a Bird

If you want to catch a bird
With a trick that cannot fail
Then take a little salt
And
   shake
      shake
         shake
            some on its tail.

Be a Circus Clown

Mom said to me,
    "You like to clown around?
    Then be a circus clown
    Since the circus is in town."

I said to Mom,
    "I love to clown around.
    I think I'll see the circus
    Since the circus is in town."

I ran to see the circus—
Couldn't wait to rush right down.
I up and joined the circus
While the circus was in town.
Now I always paint my face
Cause I'm a circus clown.
And I always see my Mom
When the circus is in town.

Now Mom says to me,
    "So you *still* clown around?
    I'm glad you joined the circus
    When the circus was in town.
    I'm *glad* you joined the circus
    To be a circus clown!"

The Alphabet Monster

I'm the Alphabet Monster
And nothing tastes better
To the Alphabet Monster
Than eating a letter.
A "j" and an "a"
And a "c" and a "k"
And the million more letters
I munch every day.

I'm hungry now.
What shall I do?
I think I'll eat
a "y"
an "o"
and a "u".

That means . . .YOU!

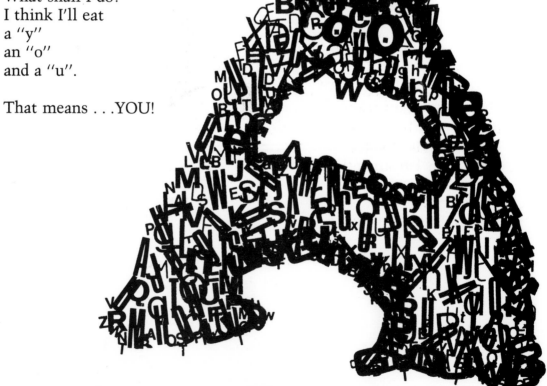

Count on Me!

You can count on me!

10 fingers and 10 toes,
2 eyes, 2 ears, 1 nose,
2 legs, 2 arms, 1 chin,
1 mouth with 30 teeth therein
2 knees, 1 front, 1 back,
1 name like Jill or Jack,
2 feet, 2 hands, 2 sides,
1 body with 1 heart inside.

Now tell me, do you see
How you can count on me?

15

Counting's Easy

Counting's easy—1 2 3
I'll count bees and chimpanzees.

Counting's easy—4 5 6
I'll count pucks and hockey sticks.

Counting's easy—7 8 9
I'll count pigs and porcupines.

Counting's easy—
10 10 10
I'll count tigers in their dens—
If . . .
      they're sleeping very tight
      and have no teeth so they can't bite
      and have no claws so they can't maul
      and if like kittens they are small.
Then . . .
I'll count tigers, count them all
10 10 10
If they're small.

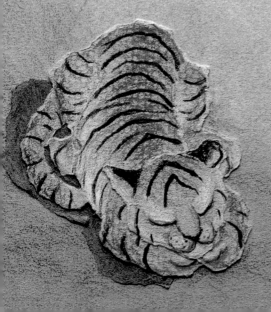

Vancouver

In Spring it sprinkles,
    In Summer too.
In Fall it pours
    Buckets on you.
In Winter it rains
    Cats and dogs
From heavy clouds
    Through soupy fogs.
All year long
    Rain drops and drops
In Vancouver
    It never stops.

Nutty Chant

Peanuts, almonds, pecans too,
Walnuts, Brazil nuts,
What do you do?

Crack them,
Shell them,
Swallow them down.
Put the shells in your socks and wiggle around.

Peanuts, almonds, pecans too,
Walnuts, Brazil nuts,
What do you do?

Crack them,
Shell them,
Swallow them down.
Put the shells in your shoes and wiggle to town.

19

Ellie the Elephant

I'm Ellie the elephant, elephant, elephant.
I'm ever so elegant, elegant, elegant.
Eggs are all I ever eat,
I won't eat cake, I won't eat meat.
But eggs are so eatable, eatable, eatable,
Eggs are unbeatable, -beatable, -beatable!
I hunt up high, or low, low, low,
It's easy to do with my trunk, you know.
I never, never, never forget,
Cause elephants don't—and yet, yet, yet,
Once I forgot to look where I sat.
Oh, how inelegant! SPLAT, SPLAT, SPLAT!
There was my lovely egg, egg, egg
Dripping down my leg, leg, leg.
YUK!

Don't Eat Spiders

Daddy said to me,
"Don't eat spiders,
Don't you dare.
They may be delicious,
But I don't care.
Don't eat spiders
Alive or dead.
Don't eat spiders,
That's what I said.
Don't eat spiders
Even in play,
Fried or mashed
Or *any* way.
Don't eat spiders,
That's what I say.
Never, ever,
That's what I say!"

But I answered Daddy,
"Tell me why!
Will I get sick?
Will I die?
I'll eat spiders,
I don't care.
I'll eat spiders
On a dare."

I ate a spider
Off the ground.
I swallowed a spider,
It wriggled around.

SUD-DEN-LY...
I grew eight legs,
They're skinny and hairy.
I shrank to a spider,
Creepy and scary.
I sit in a web,
I eat dead flies,
I watch the world
With eight beady eyes.

So don't eat spiders,
I hope you see,
Unless you want to be
A spider like me.
And don't eat spiders.
Do you see?
Cause if you eat spiders
You might eat ME!

23

Bird's Nest

I'm a huge, gigantic bird,
    A dinosaur in air.
I search for little children,
    To grab them by the hair.

I grab them by the hair,
    I fly them to my tree.
I gobble them all up,
    Before they yell "Help me!"

I'm looking for you now.
    You'll find me near some day.
I'll swoop right down and
    SUDDENLY—I'll carry you away.

25

Copycat

Copycat, copycat,
Shadow's a copycat!

Out in the sun
Whenever I run,
It runs.
Whenever I twirl,
It twirls.
I curl up small.
It curls up small.
I stand up tall.
It stands up tall.

Copycat, copycat,
Shadow's a copycat.

Whenever I hide,
It hides.
I spread out wide.
It spreads out wide.
I pat my head.
It pats its head.
I fall down dead.
It falls down dead.

But when I go inside to stay,
Copycat, copycat goes away!

Sticky Maple Syrup

Sticky maple syrup
Dripping from your tree
You spread across the Prairies
     the Maritimes
     B.C.
You cover up all Canada
From sea to sticky sea.
Sticky maple syrup
Don't stick all over me.

You ooze right through my window.
You slosh around my bed.
You dribble down my pancakes
    my waffles
    and my bread.
You trickle through my hair
To my eyes, my ears, my nose.
You drip behind my knees
And run between my toes.
You fill my shoes with sticky stuff.
You soak my socks right through.
My jeans, my shirt, my underwear
Are stuck to me with you.

Sticky maple syrup
I never want to meet
A grizzly bear who's hungry
For my maple syrup feet.
So—sticky maple syrup,
Wherever you may be,
I'll lick you up,
I'll lap you up,
Before you stick to me!

29

Polar Bear Snow

At Churchill, Manitoba,
Right next to Hudson Bay,
I spied a monstrous snowball
One snowy winter day.

Snow, snow, polar bear snow!

I'd never seen a snowball
So gigantic and so round,
So huge it towered over me
Upon the frozen ground.

Snow, snow, polar bear snow!

I pushed that monster snowball,
I punched it, kicked it too,
When all at once that snowball moved—
It stretched and then it grew.

Snow, snow, polar bear snow!

It had a mouth, four giant paws,
A hundred teeth, a thousand claws,
A million strands of snow-white hair.
It growled just like a. . .POLAR BEAR!

Snow, snow, polar bear snow!

"A POLAR BEAR! HELP! HELP!" I cried.
One snap!
            One gulp!
                        I was inside!

Snow, snow, polar bear snow!

It's dark and damp inside this bear,
I've been stuck at least a year—
So hurry up to Churchill now
And GET ME OUT OF HERE!

31

A Million Valentines

I'll cut a Valentine
Just for you.
I'll cut out one,
I'll cut out two,
I'll cut out three,
I'll cut out four,
I'll cut out five—
Or maybe more.
I'll cut a hundred,
A thousand too.
I'll cut a million
Just for you.
A million million
Are too few
To say how much
I love you!

Valentine Helicopter

Look up up up
In the sky sky sky
It's the Valentine helicopter
Going by by by

It goes up up up
It goes down down down

It delivers Valentines
All around town.

33

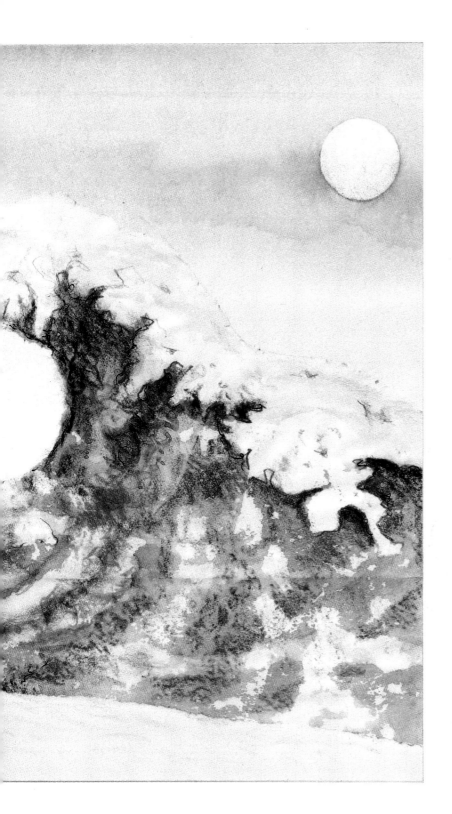

The Newfoundland Cod

Basking in the sun
One summer day
Was a giant cod
At Fortune Bay.
I stepped on this cod
In Newfoundland,
Stepped on its head
As it slept on the sand.

It sprang to its tail
By the sunny sea.
It bugged its eyes
And screamed at me:
"Kiss me or tickle me,
Hug me or pickle me,
Jiggle me, wiggle me,
Suddenly squiggle me.
Take me and flake me,
Shake me and bake me.
Batter me, fry me,
Poach me or dry me.
But keep your stinking
Feet away
From codfish sunning
At Fortune Bay!"

As it wiggled its way
Back into the sea
A monster wave
Washed over me.
It spanked me
With a dozen whacks
From Newfoundland
To Halifax.

And…
Never, ever
Since that day
Have I stepped on a cod
At Fortune Bay.

Here Comes the Witch

Here comes the witch.
        Don't make a sound.
Here comes the witch.
        Don't turn around.
Stand as still as still can be.
Like a statue, like a tree.
She's bony, warty, green-faced too,
Hungry for someone just like you.

Here comes the witch.
        She's very near.
Here comes the witch.
        She's now right here.
She's reaching out! She caught your eye!
Now raise your arms and *fly, fly, fly*!

Hallowe'en Night

I saw a ghost on Hallowe'en night.
I saw a ghost, all spooky white.

But...
        I wasn't scared.
        I knew what to do.
        I stared at that ghost,
        And I yelled "BOO!"

Up flew that ghost. It cried in fright.
It screamed and ran right out of sight.
I scared that ghost with all my might.
I scared that ghost on Hallowe'en night.

37

The Apple and the Worm

I bit an apple
    That had a worm.
I swallowed the apple,
    I swallowed the worm.
I felt it squiggle,
    I felt it squirm.
I felt it wiggle,
    I felt it turn.
It felt so slippery,
    Slimy, scummy,
I felt it land—PLOP—
    In my tummy!

I guess that worm is there to stay
Unless…
I swallow a bird some day!

Tattletale Kid

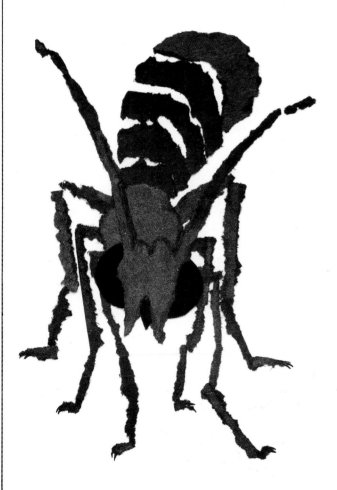

"I'm going to tell
My mom on you.
I'm going to tell
What I saw you do!"

"You'd better not tell,
You tattletale,
You'd better not tell
Or
   I'll
      stick
         a...
Bug in your ear,
Just wait and see,
A big black bug,
If you tell on me.
It'll crawl in your ear
Right to your brains.
It'll creep out
Your eyeballs
Whenever it rains.

It'll stick to your tongue
Whenever it snows.
Whenever it's hot
It'll pinch your nose.
It'll bite that nose,
Yes, eat it all.
There'll be nothing left
But a raw meatball.
Then people will point—
They'll know you told.
That bug won't die
Till you're 90 years old!

The bug's in my fist,
All ready to go.
*Are you going to tattle?
Yes or no?"*

39

The Giant Snail

"I'm hungry, hungry, hungry,"
 Said the Giant Snail.
"I could eat a horse,
 I could eat a whale.
I could eat a lion—
 Maybe even two.
I could eat a tiger
 Or I could eat YOU!"

The Casa Loma Dragon

There used to be a dragon
In the Casa Loma tower,
A fire-throwing dragon
With dreadful dragon power.

On a dark and stormy night
I sneaked into the tower
And chased that fiery dragon
To the Casa Loma shower.

Round and round the winding stairs
I chased that dragon fast,
Till I got him to the shower,
And trapped him there at last!

Then I quickly spun the faucets
In the Casa Loma shower.
I soaked the steaming dragon
And put out his fiery power.

How that dragon howled and whined
As he shot out from the shower
And raced back up the stairway
To the Casa Loma tower.

He spread his dragon wings,
Sailed flapping to the street,
And landed with a skid
On his spiky dragon feet.

He went speeding down Spadina,
Took a sharp left turn at King—
I knew I'd never catch him,
Though I ran like anything.

He went racing down the street
With all his dragon might,
When suddenly he stopped—
He'd seen a flashing light.

He laughed a dragon laugh
(It made a fearful sound),
He stretched his dragon wings
And took off from the ground.

Now the Casa Loma dragon
That I soaked in the shower
Is living at the top
Of the flashing CN Tower!

Rockets

Rockets flying out in space,
Rockets flying every place,
Rockets from Earth
　　　　to Venus and Mars,
　　　　　to silver moons and shining stars,
Rockets to galaxies far away,
I think I'll build a rocket some day.
I'll fuel it first.
I'll fly it away.
I'll land in time for Christmas day,
On Pluto, Neptune, Saturn or Mars,
On a silver moon
Or a shining star.

Space

Space is...

Planets like Pluto, Jupiter and Mars,
The Milky Way and billions of stars,
Rockets, space ships, UFOS,
Mean, ugly creatures with 36 toes.
Black holes, moons, and solar rays,
Dark cold places without any days,
Robots, space stations, laser guns,
Different galaxies with different suns.

Space is a place I'd love to see
If hungry monsters won't eat me.

Creature from Outer Space

"I come from outer space,
And I don't like your face."

"So what?
   Creature, Creature, you don't scare me!
   I have teeth.   I can bite.
   I have fists.   I can fight.
   Creature, Creature, you don't scare me!

   I've a mouth.   I can talk.
   I have legs.   I can walk.
   Creature, Creature, you don't scare me!

   I have brains.   I can think.
   I have knees.   I can shrink.
   Creature, Creature you don't scare me!

   I have hands.   I can clap.
   I have fingers.   I can snap.
   Creature, Creature, you don't scare me!

   I have feet.   I can kick.
   I have arms.   I am quick.
   Creature, Creature you don't scare me!

   I am strong.   I am rough.
   I am brave.   I am tough.
   So go away and leave me be,
   Cause Creature, Creature,
   YOU DON'T SCARE ME!

   Not at all!
   SCAT!"

Today and Yesterday

The wind blew hard
It blew me away
It blew me back to yesterday
It blew tomorrow to today
It blew today to yesterday
It blew me to this day behind
It blew me to another time

Now I'm stuck in yesterday
And there I guess I'll have to stay
Until it blows me back away
Until it blows me to today